Money 101

Let's Talk About Money

Written by

Dr. Richard L. Ferguson

Illustrated by Jera Carrera
Coins & Bills by Rachael K. Hartman

published by

Fox Tales Children's Books

a part of
Our Written Lives, LLC
in San Antonio, Texas

www.OurWrittenLives.com

Library of Congress Cataloging-in-Publication Data

Richard Ferguson

Money 101: Let's Talk About Money

Library of Congress Control Number 2023920727

ISBN 978-1-942923-67-1 (paperback)

I would like to dedicate this book to:

My Lord and Savior, Jesus Christ.

My parents.
God blessed me to be born into their family.
They taught me to love the Lord.

To my siblings.
Thank you for always giving me wise advice.

To my future wife and family.
I love you and thank God for you before you are here.

Money Talk!

Money comes in two forms.
Money comes in coins.
Money comes in paper bills.

Making Money!

We work to earn money.

Can kids earn money? Yes, you can!

What are some jobs around your house
or neighborhood you can do to earn money?

CHORES
25¢
sweep
pick up toys

Saving Money!

Can kids save money? **Yes, you can!**

Here is an easy way to save money.
1. Get three jars with lids.
2. Label the jars: saving, giving, and spending.

We **save** money for important things we need to buy.
We **give** money to help people in need.
We **spend** money on things we need or want.

What is a need? What is a want?

Spending Money!

We use money to buy goods or services.
What are goods? What are services?
Can you think of some goods and services?

COINS & BILLS

The Penny

The first piece of money we will look at is the penny. The penny is equal to one cent.

We can write one cent in two ways:
$0.01 or 1¢.

It takes 100 pennies to make one dollar!

On the front of the penny, we can see the picture of the 16th president of the United States, Abraham Lincoln.

On the back of the penny are pictures of the Lincoln Memorial and the Lincoln Shield.

Can you find a penny with the Lincoln Shield on it?

The penny used to be made of copper Pennies made before 1980 were made of copper, but the new ones are made of zinc.

All pennies are a copper color when new and clean, and more of a brown color when older and dirty.

The Nickel

The second piece of money we will look at is the nickel. A nickel is equal to five cents, or five pennies.

We can write one nickle as:
$0.05 or 5¢.

It takes 20 nickels to make one dollar! The nickel is a silver color.

On the front of the nickel is Thomas Jefferson. He was the third president of the United States.

On the back of the nickel is Monticello, Thomas Jefferson's home located in Virginia.

Five pennies is also equal to $0.05, the same amount as a nickel is worth.

The Dime

The third piece of money we will look at is the dime. A dime is equal to ten cents, or ten pennies.

We can write ten cents in two ways:
$0.10 or 10¢.

On the front of the dime is Franklin D. Roosevelt. He was the 32nd president of the United States.

On the back of the dime are an olive branch, a torch, and an oak branch. The dime is silver in color.

Ten pennies equals $0.10, the same amount as a dime is worth.

The Quarter

The forth piece of money is the quarter. The quarter equals twenty-five cents. It is bigger than pennies, nickles, or dimes. The quarter is silver in color.

We can write a quarter in two ways: **$0.25 or 0.25¢.**

On the front of the Washington Quarter is the first President of the United States, George Washington. He may be facing the left or the right.

On the back of the Washington Quarter is an eagle, the drummer boy, or a scene representing one of the 50 states or national parks. There is also a series featuring American women. Maya Angelou was the first woman featured on a quarter.

All quarters are the same size.

Two dimes and a nickel equal $0.25, the same amount as a quarter. How else can you create $0.25 using other coins?

The Half-Dollar

The fifth piece of money is the half-dollar or fifty-cent piece. The fifty-cent piece is equal to fifty cents, which is the same as: fifty pennies, ten nickels, five dimes, or two quarters.

We can write fifty cents in two ways: **$0.50 or 0.50¢**.

On the front of the fifty-cent piece is the 35th President of the United States, John F. Kennedy.

On the back of the fifty-cent piece is the presidential seal.

The fifty-cent piece is silver in color.

The half-dollar, or fifty-cent piece, is worth the same amount of money as two quarters, or $0.50.

What other coin combinations can you create $0.50 with?

The Gold Dollar

The sixth piece of money is the gold dollar. The gold dollar is a coin and it equals one dollar. The gold dollar coin is a gold color.

We write the gold dollar the same way as a paper dollar: **$1.00**.

Some gold dollar coins have Lady Liberty on the front with the number one, and the year 1849 on the back. 1849 is the year the gold dollar coin was designed.

Other gold dollars feature the famous Native American Indian guide, Sacajawea. On the back of those gold dollars is a flying eagle.

A gold dollar is worth the same amount of money as a one dollar bill, or as four quarters, or two fifty-cent pieces.

What other coins can be combined to make $1?

One Dollar Bill

The seventh piece of money is the one dollar bill. The one dollar bill is equal to one dollar, 100 pennies, 20 nickels, 10 dimes, or 4 quarters.

We write one dollar bill as: **$1.00**.

On the front of the one dollar bill is the 1st President of the United States, George Washington.

On the back of the one dollar bill is the great seal of the United States. The one dollar bill is green and white.

Two Dollar Bill

The eighth piece of money is the two-dollar bill. The two dollar bill is equal to two dollars.

We write two dollars as: **$2.00.**

On the front of the two-dollar bill is Thomas Jefferson, the third president of the United States. He's the same man on the nickel.

On the back of the two-dollar bill is a picture of a painting by John Trumbull. The painting is titled: The Declaration of Independence, July 4, 1776. The two-dollar bill is green and white in color.

Five Dollar Bill

The ninth piece of money is the five-dollar bill. The five-dollar bill is worth five one-dollar bills.

We write five dollars as: **$5.00**.

On the front of the five-dollar bill is the 16th President of the United States, Abraham Lincoln.

On the back of the five-dollar bill is the Lincoln Memorial.

What does the five-dollar bill's design remind us of? That's right, the penny!

The five-dollar bill is green and white, and some places may have a purple tone.

Ten Dollar Bill

The tenth piece of money is the ten-dollar bill. The ten-dollar bill is equal to ten dollars.

We write ten dollars as: **$10.00**.

On the front of the ten-dollar bill is the first Secretary of the Treasury, Alexander Hamilton.

On the back of the ten-dollar bill is the United States Treasury.

The ten-dollar bill is green and white and may have some parts in red or gold.

Twenty-Dollar Bill

The eleventh piece of money is the twenty-dollar bill. The twenty-dollar bill equals twenty dollars.

We write twenty dollars as: **$20.00**.

On the front of the twenty-dollar bill is the 17th President of the United States, Andrew Jackson.

On the back of the twenty-dollar bill is the White House in Washington D.C. *Who lives in the White House?* That's right, whoever is the current President of the United States lives there.

The twenty-dollar bill is green and white and may have some blue, orange, or gold.

Fifty-Dollar Bill

The twelfth piece of money is the fifty-dollar bill. The fifty-dollar bill is worth fifty dollars.

We write fifty dollars as: **$50.00**.

On the front of the fifty-dollar bill is the 18th President of the United States, Ulysses S. Grant. On the back of the fifty-dollar bill is the United States Capitol Building.

The fifty-dollar bill is green and white and may have some red on it.

One-Hundred-Dollar Bill

The thirteenth, and final piece of money we will talk about today is the one-hundred-dollar bill.

The one-hundred-dollar bill is worth one hundred dollars.

We write one-hundred-dollars as: **$100.00**

On the front of the one-hundred-dollar bill is an American Founding Father, Benjamin Franklin. He was one of the men who signed the Declaration of Independence.

On the back of the one-hundred-dollar bill is Independence Hall. The new one-hundred-dollar bill is a pale blue color, but older versions are green and white with orange and red in some places.

MONEY MATH!

Counting money is a fun way for children to learn math.
Money can be added, subtracted, divided, and multiplied.

Let's try some Money Math!

$1 + $2 = _____
$5 - $2 = _____
$100 / $50 = _____
$10 x $10.00 = _____

1/4 of a dollar is = 0.25¢ or one quarter
1/2 of a dollar is = 0.50¢ or two quarters
1/3 of a dollar is = 0.75¢ or three quarters

Counting Money!

Counting money is an important skill that every person can learn to do. When you are familiar with each coin and bill, you will be able to count money very quickly.

It's also a good idea to be familiar with what coin combinations equal $1, $2, etc. It can be fun to think of all of the ways we can combine coins and bills to equal the same amount.

What coins or bills make one dollar?

100 pennies
20 nickels
10 dimes
4 quarters
2 half dollars (fifty-cent pieces)
1 gold dollar coin
1 dollar bill

What coins or bills make two dollars?

200 pennies
40 nickels
20 dimes
8 quarters
4 half-dollars
2 gold dollar coins
2 one dollar bills

What coins or bills make five dollars?

500 pennies
100 nickels
50 dimes
20 quarters
10 half-dollars
5 gold dollar coins
5 one dollar bills

What coins or bills make ten dollars?

1,000 pennies
200 nickels
100 dimes
40 quarters
20 half-dollars, or fifty-cent pieces
10 gold dollar coins
10 one-dollar bills
1 ten dollar bill

What coins or bills make twenty dollars?

2,000 pennies
400 nickels
200 dimes
80 quarters
45 fifty-cent pieces or half dollars
20 gold coins
20 one-dollar bills
4 five-dollar bills
2 ten-dollar bills
1 twenty-dollar bill

What coins or bills makes fifty dollars?

5,000 pennies
1,000 nickels
500 dimes
200 quarters
100 half dollars
50 gold dollar coins
50 one dollar bills
25 two-dollar bills
10 five dollar bills
5 ten dollar bills
1 fifty dollar bill

What coins or bills makes one hundred dollars?

10,0000 pennies
2,000 nickels
1,000 dimes
400 quarters
200 half-dollars
100 gold dollar coins
100 one dollar bills
50 two-dollar bills
20 five dollar bills
10 ten-dollar bills
5 twenty-dollar bills
2 fifty-dollar bills
1 one-hundred dollar bill

About the Author
Dr. Richard L. Ferguson

Dr. Richard L. Ferguson is a Pastor, business owner, and the author of News Letters Chronicles an Encouragement Devotional, written to encourage everyone in this complex life. He lives in Ridgeland, South Carolina.

Money 101: Let's Talk About Money is a needed tool to teach children about money, its importance in math, as well as a little bit of history about the cash and change we use every day. This book teaches children how to recognize coins and bills used in the United States.

Dr. Ferguson believes educating the future generation from a young age will equip them to start thinking about money and how it works earlier, and will help change the future of our economy.

You can reach Dr. Ferguson at heavensgates12@yahoo.com, or connect on his Facebook page by searching for Dr. Richard L. Ferguson.

About the Illustrator
Jera Carrera

Hi! I'm Jera Carrera, a freelance artist from Sugartown, Louisiana. I'm a devoted wife to my husband Gustavo and a mother of three beautiful miracles.

My Grannie Ford and my parents encouraged my love for drawing ever since I was very young. In school, I took every art class I could, painting lessons during summers, and eventually, I went on to study Art and Art Education at McNeese State University.

Art took a back burner for many years, but I've finally found my spark again. In 2022, I started *Jera Carrera Freelance Art* and began taking portrait commissions. I've expanded to offer book illustration services and other special projects. One day, I plan to write and illustrate my very own books!

You can find me on Facebook by looking for my page, *Jera Carrera Freelance Art.*

About the Illustrator
Rachael K. Hartman

Hello! I'm Rachael and I created the coins and bills you see throughout this book. This project was an incredible journey with challenges along the way. I'm honored to say it's the very first book I personally assisted in creating art for. I've always loved art, but my strength lies in writing and editing.

In fact, I published this book and several others through my publishing business Fox Tales Children's Books, a division of my larger company Our Written Lives, LLC.

I love helping authors achieve their dreams. I get to work with great people like Dr. Richard Ferguson, whom I met a few years ago, and Jera Carrera, my long-time friend.

I've now worked with nearly 80 books, and I talk to new authors all of the time. I've written five books of my own and I am excited to say I'm working on my first children's book project, which should be completed soon. I also have plans for a children's book series that has been in my heart for many years.

You can learn more about me, my books, and the authors I work with, by visiting my professional portfolio or business site, both listed below. I'm also on Facebook, Instagram, TikTok, and YouTube under by business name, Our Written Lives.

www.RachaelKHartman.com

www.OurWrittenLives.com

Fox Tales Children's Books

OUR WRITTEN LIVES
Book Publishing & Writing Services

www.OurWrittenLives.com

www.ingramcontent.com/pod-product-compliance
Lightning Source LLC
Chambersburg PA
CBRC090851210326
41597CB00011B/166